THE OXO® COOKBOOK

QUADRILLE

Photography by
Ria Osborne

PUBLISHING DIRECTOR Sarah Lavelle
SENIOR EDITOR Céline Hughes
COPY EDITOR Sally Somers
CREATIVE DIRECTOR Helen Lewis
ART DIRECTION AND DESIGN Katherine Keeble
ASSISTANT DESIGNER Gemma Hayden
PHOTOGRAPHER Ria Osborne
RECIPE DEVELOPER AND FOOD STYLIST
Rukmini Iyer
PROPS STYLIST Holly Bruce
PRODUCTION DIRECTOR Vincent Smith
PRODUCTION CONTROLLER Tom Moore

First published in 2015 by Quadrille Publishing

Quadrille is an imprint of Hardie Grant
www.hardiegrant.com.au

Quadrille Publishing
Pentagon House
52–54 Southwark Street
London SE1 1UN
www.quadrille.co.uk

Cataloguing in Publication Data: a catalogue record for this book is available from the British Library.

ISBN: 978 1 84949 768 8

Printed in China

STOCKING THE NATION

For more than a century, OXO has been transforming mealtimes and helping make good food taste great.

From humble beginnings to beloved national brand, OXO has always put family first. Our iconic stock cube has been held in great affection since even before British soldiers in the First World War were given the cubes in their ration kits. 'Be sure to send OXO!' was our advertising slogan, and we hoped to provide a little warmth and comfort to our soldiers, far from their families and missing home.

Our first TV adverts in the 1950s saw 'Katie' using beef stock cubes to make mid-week meals for the family. She demonstrated the versatility and convenience of OXO that continues to resonate today. Fast forward a couple of decades and the most famous TV 'family' must surely be Lynda Bellingham's, in the hugely popular 1980s and '90s adverts. Her family and home become the fond symbol of OXO.

Throughout the years, cooks across the country have relied on us to make their cooking simply delicious. So, even though times have changed and the world is more fast-paced, we're proud to continue to be one of the most used and most recognised ingredients in the kitchen.

Today, our range of products has grown to meet changing tastes. As well as stock cubes in assorted flavours, other ingredients have been developed to help modern, busy cooks make fresh, tasty meals with minimum fuss.

This cookbook will show you just how much you can do with OXO – there's a recipe here for every occasion. From simple soups and convenient mid-week meals from around the world, to show-stopping Sunday roasts and one-pot wonders – there's so much to enjoy.

Now it's time to get into the kitchen and get cooking! With a pinch of effort, a splash of creativity and a sprinkle of OXO, you can feed friends and family fast, fabulous food.

ox

1

SOUPS

CARROT AND BEETROOT SOUP (V)

This healthy soup is quick to prepare and, with its minty notes and vibrant colour, makes a lovely lunch in mid-to-late summer, when beetroot are at their best. Serve with crusty bread.

20g butter
a glug of olive oil
3 fresh thyme sprigs
325g carrots, grated
300g raw beetroot, peeled and grated
2 x OXO Garden Vegetables with Parsley & Bay Stock Pots, made up with 850ml boiling water
a large handful of fresh mint leaves, plus extra sprigs to serve
a squeeze of lemon juice, or to taste
sea salt and freshly ground black pepper
4 dollops of Greek yoghurt, to serve

1 Heat the butter and olive oil together in a large saucepan, add the thyme and fry for a few seconds until aromatic, then add the carrots and beetroot. Stir well, cover and cook for 15 minutes to soften, stirring just occasionally.

2 Add the OXO stock and simmer for 10 minutes, then add the mint, remove any woody thyme sprigs and blitz until smooth, using a hand-held blender or in a food processor. Add a little more OXO stock to thin the soup if you wish.

3 Add a squeeze of lemon juice and a pinch of salt and pepper to taste. Serve hot in bowls or cups, with a dollop of Greek yoghurt and a sprig of mint.

PEA AND MINT
SOUP (V)

Incredibly quick to prepare, this soup brings all the fresh flavours of summer to the table. On really hot days, make it ahead and chill it for several hours before serving with crusty bread for an elegant first course for dinner, or a light lunch with friends.

a glug of olive oil
4 spring onions, finely sliced
4 garlic cloves, finely chopped
400g defrosted frozen peas
2 x OXO Garden Vegetables with Parsley & Bay Stock Pots, made up with 700ml boiling water
a very large handful of fresh mint leaves, plus extra to serve
a big squeeze of lemon juice, or to taste
sea salt and freshly ground black pepper

1 Heat the oil in a large saucepan, add the spring onions and garlic and fry for 2–3 minutes before adding the peas, OXO stock and mint.

2 Bring to the boil and simmer for 2 minutes, then blitz until smooth using a hand-held blender or in a food processor.

3 Add a big squeeze of lemon juice, a scattering of mint leaves, and a pinch of salt and pepper to taste, and serve hot or chilled.

QUICK FRENCH ONION SOUP (V)

The croutons, with the cheese bubbling on top, add wonderful texture and body to this comforting dish, transforming the delicate broth into a warming, satisfying winter lunch.

30g butter
a glug of olive oil
800g onions (about 4 large), thinly sliced
1 teaspoon caster sugar
150ml white wine
2 x OXO Garden Vegetables with Parsley & Bay Stock Pots, made up with 1 litre boiling water
sea salt and freshly ground black pepper

For the croutons
4 slices of baguette
35g grated Cheddar cheese

1 Heat the butter and oil together in a large saucepan until the butter stops foaming. Add the onions and cook over a medium to high heat for 10 minutes, stirring occasionally.

2 Add the sugar, stir well, then reduce the heat to medium low and leave to caramelise for 10 minutes, stirring occasionally.

3 Add the wine and bubble it down for 3–4 minutes, scraping the base of the pan well with a wooden spoon to release any sediment. Add the OXO stock, stir well, bring to the boil and simmer over a high heat for 15 minutes.

4 Meanwhile, for the croutons, lightly toast the baguette slices on both sides under a medium grill. Just before the soup is ready, sprinkle grated cheese over each slice and place under the grill until the cheese is bubbling and evenly browned.

5 Add a pinch of salt and pepper to taste and serve in warmed bowls, with a cheese-topped crouton floating in each.

CORN CHOWDER

SERVES
4

PREP TIME
5–10 MINUTES

COOKING TIME
20 MINUTES

This very simple and quick recipe produces a wonderfully creamy chowder, with the unblended mixture adding a great texture to the finished dish. Ideal for a really satisfying weekend family lunch.

140g diced pancetta
6 spring onions, finely sliced
100g celery, finely chopped
2 garlic cloves, finely chopped
2 x 340g tins sweetcorn, drained, or 570g frozen sweetcorn, defrosted
400ml milk
1 x OXO Succulent Chicken with Garlic & Thyme Stock Pot, made up with 500ml boiling water
a big squeeze of lemon juice, or to taste
sea salt and freshly ground black pepper

1 Heat a large saucepan, add the pancetta and fry over a low heat for 3–4 minutes before adding the spring onions, celery and garlic.

2 Stir well, cover and cook for 5 minutes to soften, then add the sweetcorn, milk and OXO stock.

3 Simmer for 10 minutes, then pour half the mixture into a measuring jug or food processor and blitz until smooth using a hand-held blender, or in the processor. Return the blended mixture to the pan and stir well.

4 Season well with a big squeeze of lemon juice and a pinch of salt and pepper, and serve hot.

SPICY BUTTERNUT SQUASH SOUP (V)

The ginger and chilli give this velvety soup a bit of a kick, with the creamy coconut milk balancing out the flavours. Serve with crusty bread for a filling lunch.

a glug of olive oil
1 large onion, roughly chopped
a small knob of fresh ginger, peeled and chopped
½ red chilli, finely chopped
2 garlic cloves, finely chopped
900g butternut squash, peeled, deseeded and cut into 1cm chunks
1 x OXO Garden Vegetables with Parsley & Bay Stock Pot, made up with 500ml boiling water
400ml coconut milk
2–3 tablespoons chopped fresh coriander, to serve

1 Heat the oil in a large saucepan, add the onion, ginger, chilli and garlic and fry for 5 minutes until softened. Add the squash, OXO stock, and all but 4 tablespoons of the coconut milk.

2 Bring to the boil, then reduce the heat and simmer for 15 minutes until the squash is cooked through. Blitz until smooth, using a hand-held blender or in a food processor, and serve hot, swirled through with the reserved coconut milk and chopped coriander.

Cook's Tip: To speed up the cooking time, cut the peeled and deseeded butternut squash into large chunks, then use a food processor to blitz it into small pieces before cooking.

CHICKEN, LIME AND CORIANDER BROTH

Our Asian-inspired broth has lovely, clean flavours, and makes a light and healthy lunch option. For a more substantial serving, add cooked rice or egg noodles to each bowl before serving.

a big glug of vegetable oil
6 spring onions, green and white parts, sliced on the diagonal
a knob of fresh ginger, peeled and grated
1 red chilli, finely sliced
4 garlic cloves, grated
finely grated zest and juice of 2 limes, plus lime wedges to serve
2 x OXO Chicken Stock Cubes, made up with 1.4 litres boiling water
2 boneless, skinless chicken breasts (about 300g)
a large handful of fresh coriander, roughly chopped
sea salt

1 Heat the oil in a large saucepan and add the spring onions, ginger, chilli, garlic and lime zest. Fry for 1 minute, then add the OXO stock and bring to the boil.

2 Add the chicken breasts and reduce the heat to a very low simmer. Cook, partially covered, for 15 minutes until the chicken is cooked through. Remove the chicken from the broth using a slotted spoon and, when cool enough to handle, shred it.

3 Return the shredded chicken to the broth, along with the lime juice and chopped coriander. Add a pinch of salt to taste, and serve hot, with the lime wedges to squeeze over.

TOMATO AND FENNEL SOUP WITH COD

This really is so quick and easy to make, but its Provençal flavours elevate it from the everyday and make it perfect to serve to friends. Try substituting other types of fish or seafood to suit what is available, and tuck in with plenty of crusty bread to mop up the juices.

a big glug of olive oil
3 garlic cloves, finely chopped
2 pared strips of lemon zest
½ teaspoon dried chilli flakes
1 onion, sliced
2 fennel bulbs, sliced (reserve the frilly tops to serve)
1 x OXO Rosemary & Thyme Herbs & More
8 large vine tomatoes, chopped
1 x OXO Garden Vegetables with Parsley & Bay Stock Pot, made up with 500ml boiling water
a big squeeze of lemon juice, or to taste
4 cod fillets (about 600g), cut into 5cm chunks
sea salt and freshly ground black pepper

1 Heat the oil in a large stock pot, then add the garlic, lemon zest and chilli flakes. Fry over a low heat for 2 minutes, then add the onion, fennel and OXO Rosemary & Thyme Herbs & More.

2 Stir well, cover and cook over a low heat for 10 minutes, stirring occasionally, until softened. Add the tomatoes and OXO stock and bring to the boil, then simmer for 10 minutes, partially covered.

3 Add a big squeeze of lemon juice and a pinch of salt and pepper to taste, then add the cod chunks. Simmer over a very low heat for 4–6 minutes until the cod is just cooked through.

4 Sprinkle over the reserved frilly fennel tops and serve at once.

TOM YUM SOUP WITH PRAWNS, MUSHROOMS AND COCONUT

This hot and aromatic Thai soup is a real taste-bud boost, ideal for a light lunch or supper on a cold winter's day.

a glug of sunflower oil
3 spring onions, halved across and finely sliced lengthways
a knob of of fresh ginger, peeled and cut into matchsticks
2–3 tablespoons tom yum paste
400ml coconut milk
1 x OXO Vegetable Stock Cube, made up with 500ml boiling water
200g oriental mushrooms, sliced if large
225g raw king prawns

1 Heat the oil in a large saucepan, add the spring onions and ginger and fry over a high heat for 2 minutes.

2 Add the tom yum paste, coconut milk and OXO stock.

3 Bring to the boil and simmer for 5 minutes, then add the mushrooms and prawns and cook for 3 minutes, until the prawns are cooked through. Serve immediately.

ox

ONE POT WONDERS

QUICK-COOK CHICKEN AND TARRAGON CASSEROLE

Tarragon, chicken and cream are natural companions and come together here in a wonderfully delicious and surprisingly quick-to-prepare dish.

a big glug of olive oil
2 onions, finely sliced
2 garlic cloves, finely chopped
1 x OXO Lemon & Thyme Herbs & More
4 boneless, skinless chicken breasts, cut into 2.5cm chunks
100ml white wine
60ml double cream
4 tablespoons chopped fresh tarragon leaves
a big squeeze of lemon juice, or to taste
sea salt and freshly ground black pepper

1 Heat the olive oil in a large frying pan and add the onions and garlic. Cover and cook over a low heat for 10 minutes. When the onions have softened, stir in the OXO Lemon & Thyme Herbs & More.

2 Add the chicken, increase the heat to medium and fry for 2–3 minutes before adding the wine and letting it bubble down for a minute. Cover and cook for 5 minutes over a low heat.

3 Stir through the cream and tarragon and cook for a further 1 minute. Season well with a big squeeze of lemon juice and a pinch of salt and pepper, and serve hot with rice or new potatoes.

SAUSAGE AND BEAN CASSEROLE

This is a real crowd-pleaser, ideal for a family meal. It can be ready in no time at all, for a busy midweek supper, but if you have more time to spare, it is even better left on the stove to simmer gently for up to an hour, adding more stock as needed.

a big glug of olive oil
8 good-quality pork sausages
2 onions, finely sliced
3 garlic cloves, finely chopped
½ teaspoon dried chilli flakes
1 x OXO Rosemary & Thyme Herbs & More
400g tin chopped tomatoes
1 x OXO Succulent Chicken with Garlic & Thyme Stock Pot, made up with 500ml boiling water
2 x 175g tins haricot beans, drained and rinsed
sea salt and freshly ground black pepper
a handful of freshly torn basil, to serve (optional)

1 Heat half the oil in a large frying pan, add the sausages and fry for 5–6 minutes, turning every couple of minutes, until golden brown all over.

2 Meanwhile, in a second frying pan, heat the remaining oil and add the onions, garlic and chilli flakes. Cover and cook over a low heat for 10 minutes, stirring occasionally, until the onions have softened.

3 Tip the onions into the pan with the sausages. Add the OXO Rosemary & Thyme Herbs & More, tomatoes, the OXO stock and drained haricot beans. Bring to the boil and simmer, uncovered, for 20 minutes, stirring occasionally.

4 Add a pinch of salt and pepper to taste, stir through the basil, if using, and serve hot.

MUSHROOM STROGANOFF (V)

If you can seek out the more unusual mushroom varieties, this dish can look very elegant and pretty, and is perfect for serving to vegetarian friends, either on toast for a casual lunch, or with rice or pasta for a more complete meal.

500g mixed mushrooms, such as portabellini, chestnut, button, oyster or shiitake
40g butter
a glug of olive oil
3 garlic cloves, crushed
3 tablespoons chopped fresh tarragon
1 x OXO Lemon & Thyme Herbs & More
100ml white wine
100ml double cream
a big squeeze of lemon juice, or to taste
sea salt and freshly ground black pepper

1 Halve, quarter or slice the mushrooms according to size, leaving any smaller ones whole.

2 Heat the butter and oil together in a large frying pan and add the garlic as soon as the butter stops foaming. Add the chopped tarragon and the OXO Lemon & Thyme Herbs & More and stir well until melted, before adding the mushrooms.

3 Fry for 6–7 minutes until the mushrooms start to look cooked, but still retain some bite, then add the wine and let it bubble down for 2–3 minutes before adding the cream.

4 Cook gently for a further 2 minutes, then remove from the heat. Add a big squeeze of lemon juice and a pinch of salt and pepper to taste, before serving hot.

IRISH STEW

This hearty stew is a great winter warmer and involves minimal work, looking after itself nicely in the oven. With veg and potatoes integral to the dish, you don't even need to prepare anything to go on the side – a true one pot wonder.

a big glug of olive oil
400g lamb neck, cut into 3cm chunks
140g bacon lardons
2 large onions, roughly chopped
300g carrots, roughly sliced
300g celery, roughly chopped
2 x OXO Rich Beef with Onion & Rosemary Stock Pots, made up with 800ml boiling water
400g floury potatoes, such as Maris Piper, peeled and cut into 2cm chunks
sea salt and freshly ground black pepper

1 Preheat the oven to 160°C/gas 3. Heat half the oil in a large flameproof casserole. Season the lamb well on all sides with salt and pepper and, working in batches, fry on all sides for about 5 minutes, until well browned, adding the remaining oil as needed.

2 Remove the browned lamb to a plate using a slotted spoon, and, in the same casserole, fry the bacon for 3–4 minutes until crisp. Add the onions, carrot and celery and fry for a further 5 minutes, until softened.

3 Return the meat to the casserole with the vegetables and add the hot OXO stock and potatoes. Cover with a lid and transfer to the oven to cook for 2 hours. Season to taste and serve hot.

Cook's Tip: If you don't have a lidded flameproof casserole, fry the lamb and vegetables in a large frying pan before transferring everything into an ovenproof dish. Cover with 2 layers of foil before transferring to the oven.

PORK, CIDER AND APPLE STEW

This lovely autumnal dish with its classic combination of pork and apple makes an excellent weekend lunch or dinner, served with mashed or baked potatoes.

800g diced pork shoulder
2 tablespoons plain flour
a big glug of olive oil
300ml dry cider
30g butter
2 onions, roughly sliced
200g celery, roughly sliced
2 sharp dessert apples, such as Granny Smith, cored and cut into large chunks
1 x OXO Succulent Chicken with Garlic & Thyme Stock Pot, made up with 400ml boiling water
sea salt and freshly ground black pepper
chopped fresh parsley, to serve

1 Preheat the oven to 150°C/gas 2. Dust the diced pork pieces with the flour and season well with salt and pepper.

2 Heat half the oil in a large frying pan. Working in batches, fry the pork for 2 minutes on each side until well browned, using the remaining oil as needed. Transfer to a bowl.

3 Pour the cider into the same pan and let it bubble down for a few minutes, scraping up any sediment from the base using a wooden spoon. Tip the contents of the pan over the pork.

4 Melt the butter in a large flameproof casserole and add the onions, celery and apple. Stir well, cover with the lid and cook over a low heat for 10 minutes, until softened.

5 Add the pork to the casserole with the OXO stock. Season well with salt and pepper, bring to the boil then cover and transfer immediately to the oven. Cook for 2 hours, then garnish with parsley and enjoy with roast potatoes.

RATATOUILLE (V)

This updated French summer dish, with its attractive overlapping layers, makes a delicious accompaniment to meat, fish or egg dishes. Or simply serve with crusty bread and perhaps a green salad, for a late summer or early autumn lunch.

4 tablespoons olive oil
1 red onion, thinly sliced
1 red pepper, deseeded and thinly sliced
3 garlic cloves, thinly sliced
1 x OXO Rosemary & Thyme Herbs & More
6 large, ripe vine tomatoes (about 900g), roughly chopped
1 large aubergine, very thinly sliced into rounds
1 large courgette, very thinly sliced into rounds
sea salt and freshly ground black pepper

1 Preheat the oven to 180°C/gas 4.

2 Heat half the oil in a large frying pan and add the onion, red pepper and garlic. Add a pinch of salt and cook over a medium to low heat for 15 minutes to soften, stirring frequently.

3 Add the OXO Rosemary & Thyme Herbs & More and tomatoes and stir well to dissolve. Increase the heat and bring to a gentle simmer before covering and cooking for 15 minutes.

4 Remove the lid and cook for a further 5 minutes, uncovered, before seasoning to taste with a little salt and pepper.

5 In a round or oval ovenproof dish, about 18cm diameter, overlap the aubergine and courgette slices in a single layer before adding a thin layer of tomato sauce. Repeat the layers, seasoning each layer of aubergines and courgettes, until you have used up all the vegetables, finishing with a layer of aubergine and courgette slices.

6 Drizzle generously with the remaining oil, sprinkle with salt and transfer to the oven to bake for 45 minutes. Serve hot.

CHICKEN AND CHORIZO PAELLA

This simple but delicious adaptation of the Spanish classic is ideal for a lunch with friends or family; put the pan in the middle of the table for everyone to help themselves, and serve with crusty bread and/or a green salad.

a big glug of olive oil
140g chorizo, chopped
2 red onions, thickly sliced
4 red peppers, deseeded and thickly sliced
6 garlic cloves, crushed
700g boneless, skinless chicken thighs, cut into quarters
4 teaspoons smoked paprika
500g paella rice, rinsed
3 x OXO Succulent Chicken with Garlic & Thyme Stock Pots, made up with 1.8 litres boiling water
a big squeeze of lemon juice, or to taste
sea salt and freshly ground black pepper
a handful of fresh flat-leaf parsley, chopped, to serve

1 Heat the oil in a very large frying pan, add the chorizo and fry over a low heat for 2 minutes. Add the onions and cook, stirring, for 5 minutes.

2 Add the peppers and garlic and cook, stirring, for a further 5–6 minutes until softened. Add the chicken and smoked paprika and cook for a further 2 minutes.

3 Add the rice and cook, stirring, for 2 minutes, to toast it and coat it well in the cooking oil. Pour in the OXO stock and stir well, then simmer for 20 minutes until the rice is cooked, stirring every 5 minutes to ensure even cooking.

4 Add a big squeeze of lemon juice and a pinch of salt and pepper to taste, adding a little more OXO stock to adjust the consistency if required. Sprinkle over the parsley before serving.

SPRING VEGETABLE 'ORZOTTO' (V)

This speedy and easy risotto-type dish is made not with rice but with orzo, the tiny rice-shaped pasta often used in soups or salads. Serve with a simple green salad for a weekday supper or weekend lunch.

2 x OXO Garden Vegetables with Parsley & Bay Stock Pots
400g orzo pasta
100g defrosted frozen peas
a glug of olive oil
1 onion, finely chopped
150g leeks, finely sliced
50g celery, finely chopped
50ml white wine
50g Parmesan, grated
a big squeeze of lemon juice, or to taste
sea salt and freshly ground black pepper

1 Bring 3 litres water to the boil in a large pan. Add the OXO Garden Vegetables with Parsley & Bay Stock Pots. Add the orzo and simmer for 10 minutes, adding the peas for the final 2 minutes.

2 Meanwhile, heat the oil in a large saucepan and add the onion. Cook for 5 minutes to soften, then add the leeks and celery, cover and cook for a further 5 minutes, until softened.

3 Pour in the wine and bubble it down for a couple of minutes, stirring constantly. Drain the hot orzo, retaining a few ladlefuls of the cooking stock, and add the orzo and peas to the softened vegetables.

4 Stir well and add the reserved stock a little at a time, until you have an oozy, risotto-like consistency. Stir in the Parmesan, check the seasoning and add a big squeeze of lemon juice and a pinch of salt and pepper to taste, before serving immediately.

ox

3

AROUND THE WORLD

LAMB AND APRICOT TAGINE

The flavours of this fragrant dish, with the sweetness from the apricots and the richness from the lamb, meld together beautifully as it cooks in the oven. Served with rice, couscous or flatbreads, it makes a perfect dinner to share with friends.

500g lamb neck or stewing steak, cut into large chunks
3 tablespoons olive oil
2 teaspoons cumin seeds
2 large onions, finely chopped
4 garlic cloves, finely chopped
2 teaspoons ground coriander
1 teaspoon ground cinnamon
400g tin chopped tomatoes
1 x OXO Lamb Stock Cube, made up with 300ml boiling water
200g dried apricots
sea salt and freshly ground black pepper
a handful of fresh coriander leaves, to serve

1 Preheat the oven to 170°C/gas 3½. Season the lamb well on all sides with salt and pepper.

2 Heat 1 tablespoon of the oil in a large flameproof casserole and, working in 2 or 3 batches, brown the lamb on all sides for about 5 minutes, adding another tablespoon of oil as necessary. Remove the browned lamb to a plate.

3 Heat the remaining tablespoon of oil in the casserole, add the cumin seeds and fry for over a low heat for a few seconds until aromatic, then add the onions and fry over a medium heat for 10 minutes until crisp and golden brown.

4 Add the garlic, ground coriander and cinnamon and fry over a low heat for 2 minutes. Add the tomatoes, OXO stock, apricots and browned lamb, stir well, then put the lid on and transfer to the oven to cook for 2 hours. Serve hot, sprinkled with the coriander leaves.

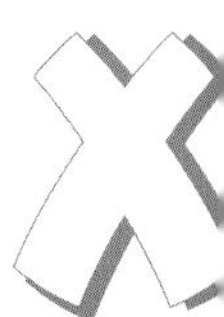

MOROCCAN CHICKEN STEW

Using mainly storecupboard ingredients and taking minimal time to prepare, this fragrant dish makes an ideal supper on a busy day. Serve with toasted flatbreads or pitta, or couscous.

2 lemons
a big glug of olive oil
2 onions, finely sliced
6 garlic cloves, finely chopped
2 teaspoons ground coriander
2 teaspoons ground cumin
2 teaspoons cayenne
1 scant teaspoon ground turmeric
700g boneless, skinless chicken breasts, cut into 4cm chunks
1 x OXO Chicken Stock Cube, made up with 400ml boiling water
100g black olives
sea salt

To serve
a handful of fresh coriander leaves, finely chopped
lemon wedges (optional)

1 Using a vegetable peeler, pare the zest of 1 of the lemons into 6 strips, then squeeze the juice and set aside. Cut the remaining lemon into slices and set aside.

2 Heat the oil in a large frying pan and add the onions, garlic and pared lemon zest. Fry over a medium heat for 5 minutes, stirring occasionally, until the onions are golden brown.

3 Reduce the heat, add the ground coriander, cumin, cayenne and turmeric and fry for 2 minutes. Increase the heat and add the chicken. Fry for 2–3 minutes, then add the OXO stock, olives and slices of lemon.

4 Bring to the boil, then reduce to a gentle simmer and cook, partially covered, for 20 minutes, removing the lid for the final 10 minutes of cooking time.

5 Add the reserved lemon juice and salt to taste, then served sprinkled with the chopped coriander, and lemon wedges if you like.

COQ AU VIN

This French classic is perfect for almost any occasion and time of year, from a family midweek supper or Sunday lunch, to entertaining friends. Serve with new potatoes in summer or mashed potatoes in winter, with a veg, such as green beans, on the side.

a big glug of olive oil
1.2kg chicken thighs and drumsticks, skin on
200ml red wine
140g bacon lardons
12 shallots, peeled, and halved unless small
300g baby chestnut mushrooms
4 garlic cloves, finely chopped
2 bay leaves
1 x OXO Rosemary & Red Wine Herbs & More
1 x OXO Succulent Chicken with Garlic & Thyme Stock Pot, made up with 400ml boiling water
sea salt and freshly ground black pepper

1 Preheat the oven to 160°C/gas 3.

2 Heat half the oil in a large frying pan and, working in batches, fry the chicken pieces for 3 minutes on each side over a high heat until deep golden brown all over, adding the remaining oil as necessary. Transfer the browned chicken to a flameproof casserole.

3 Add the wine to the frying pan and bubble it down well for a couple of minutes, scraping up any sediment on the base with a wooden spoon. Tip the contents of the pan over the chicken.

4 Add the lardons to the frying pan and cook over a low heat for 5 minutes to render down the fat. Increase the heat and cook for a further 5 minutes to crisp them up. Add the shallots, mushrooms, garlic and bay leaves and fry for 2 minutes before adding to the casserole with the chicken.

5 Put the OXO Rosemary & Red Wine Herbs & More in the hot OXO stock, stir to dissolve, then pour over the chicken and vegetables. Season well with salt and pepper, stir and bring to the boil. Cover and transfer immediately to the oven to cook for 1 hour, before serving hot.

CHICKPEA AND CORIANDER CURRY (V)

Quick to prepare, using storecupboard ingredients, this makes a great vegetarian midweek supper when time is short but you want plenty of flavour. Serve with plain rice or Cashew Nut Pilaf (page 104).

a glug of sunflower oil
1 teaspoon cumin seeds
1 onion, roughly chopped
2 garlic cloves, grated
a small knob of fresh ginger, peeled and grated
1 red chilli, finely chopped
1 teaspoon ground coriander
1 teaspoon ground cumin
1 red pepper, deseeded and roughly chopped
400g tin chopped tomatoes
1 x OXO Vegetable Stock Cube, made up with 500ml boiling water
240g tin chickpeas, drained and rinsed
2 tablespoons chopped fresh coriander
sea salt

1 Heat the oil in a large frying pan, add the cumin seeds and fry for 1 minute over a low heat, then add the onion and a pinch of salt. Fry for 5 minutes over a medium heat until golden brown, then add the garlic, ginger, chilli and ground coriander and cumin.

2 Fry for 2 minutes over a low heat until aromatic, then add the pepper. Fry for 7–8 minutes, stirring occasionally, until softened, before adding the tomatoes, OXO stock and chickpeas.

3 Bring to the boil then simmer, uncovered, for 15 minutes. Add salt to taste, sprinkle with the chopped coriander and serve hot.

Cook's Tip: If time permits, for an even richer flavour, make the curry in a saucepan rather than frying pan and simmer for 30–45 minutes.

CHICKEN JALFREZI

Perfect as a quick midweek supper, served with Cashew Nut Pilaf (page 104), or with a medley of Indian dishes as part of a big meal with friends. If you prefer less heat, deseed the chilli before chopping.

3 garlic cloves, grated
a knob of fresh ginger, peeled and grated
finely grated zest and juice of 2 lemons
½ teaspoon cayenne
1 teaspoon ground coriander
2 boneless, skinless chicken breasts (about 350g), cut into 1cm slices
a glug of sunflower oil
2 teaspoons cumin seeds
1 red onion, finely sliced
1 red chilli, finely chopped
1 red pepper, deseeded and finely sliced
1 yellow pepper, deseeded and finely sliced
3 tomatoes, roughly chopped
1 x OXO Chicken Stock Cube, made up with 300ml boiling water
sea salt
a handful of fresh coriander leaves, finely chopped, to serve

1 In a plastic or china bowl, mix half the garlic, ginger, lemon zest and juice with the cayenne, ground coriander and 1 teaspoon salt. Add the chicken, mix well, cover and set aside in the fridge until ready to use.

2 Heat the oil in a large frying pan and add the cumin seeds. Fry for 1 minute until aromatic, then add the onion, chilli and the remaining ginger, garlic, and lemon zest (reserving the juice). Cook for 5 minutes over a medium to high heat until golden brown, stirring occasionally.

3 Add both peppers and fry for 7–8 minutes until softened, then add the chopped tomatoes and OXO stock and simmer for 10 minutes.

4 Add the chilled chicken, stir, bring to the boil and simmer, covered, for 5–6 minutes until the chicken is cooked through. Add the remaining lemon juice with salt to taste, then stir through the chopped coriander just before serving.

Cook's Tip: If time permits, marinate the chicken in the fridge for at least an hour, or overnight.

LAMB KEEMA
CURRY

Keema is a traditional dish using minced lamb and peas, popular in Northern India, Pakistan, Nepal and Afghanistan. It is quick to prepare, and makes a good family midweek supper, but you might want to deseed the chilli if children are eating with you. Serve with rice or flatbreads.

a glug of sunflower oil
1 teaspoon cumin seeds
1 onion, finely chopped
1 green chilli, finely chopped
2 garlic cloves, grated
a knob of fresh ginger, peeled and grated
2 teaspoons ground cumin
2 teaspoons ground coriander
425g lamb mince
½ x 400g tin chopped tomatoes
1 x OXO Lamb Stock Cube, made up with
300ml boiling water
1 tablespoon brown sugar
100g defrosted frozen peas
a handful of fresh mint leaves, finely chopped,
plus extra sprigs to serve
sea salt

1 Heat the oil in a large frying pan or flameproof casserole, add the cumin seeds and fry for 1 minute until aromatic. Add the onion and chilli and fry for 5 minutes over a high heat, stirring occasionally, until golden brown, then add the garlic, ginger, ground cumin and coriander.

2 Reduce the heat and fry for 2 minutes, then add the lamb mince. Increase the heat and fry for 7–8 minutes, stirring occasionally, until evenly crisp and well browned.

3 Add the tomatoes, OXO stock and sugar, stir well and bring to the boil. Simmer for 10 minutes over a medium to high heat, adding the peas for the final 2 minutes. Stir through the mint, add salt to taste and serve hot, with mint sprigs scattered over.

Cook's Tip: For an even richer tasting keema, increase the OXO stock to 500ml and simmer very gently over a low heat for up to 30 minutes, stirring occasionally.

QUICK-COOK
MEXICAN CHILLI

Spicy and packed with flavour, Mexican food has become hugely popular recently, and is a great, convivial way of enjoying a meal with a group of friends. Serve with plenty of guacamole, sour cream and tortilla chips.

a big glug of olive oil
1 teaspoon cumin seeds
2 onions, roughly chopped
2 garlic cloves, finely chopped
500g beef mince
250g pork mince
2 teaspoons ground coriander
2 teaspoons ground cumin
2 teaspoons smoked paprika
1 teaspoon dried chilli flakes, or more to taste
400g tin chopped tomatoes
1 x OXO Rich Beef with Onion & Rosemary Stock Pot, made up with 600ml boiling water
10g dark chocolate (minimum 70% cocoa solids)
sea salt
a big handful of fresh coriander leaves, chopped, to serve

1 Heat half the oil in a large frying pan, add the cumin seeds and fry over a low heat for 1 minute until aromatic, then add the onions and garlic. Stir, then cook for 10 minutes, stirring occasionally, to soften.

2 Meanwhile, heat the remaining oil in another large frying pan and, working in batches, brown the beef and pork mince well over a high heat until golden brown and crisp, breaking it up as you go, about 6–7 minutes per batch. You may need to add a little extra oil to the pan between batches. Return the browned batches to the pan.

3 Add the ground coriander and cumin, smoked paprika and chilli flakes to the softened onions and fry for 1 minute until aromatic, before tipping the contents of the pan into the mince in the large frying pan.

4 Stir in the tomatoes and OXO stock, bring to the boil and use a wooden spoon to scrape up any sediment from the base of the pan. Simmer for 20 minutes, stirring in the chocolate in the last minute of cooking.

5 Add a pinch of salt to taste, sprinkle on the coriander and serve.

THREE-BEAN CHILLI FAJITAS (V)

Like the Quick-cook Mexican Chilli on page 61, this is ideal for serving to groups of friends, with the dishes all arranged in the middle of the table for everyone to help themselves. If you prefer less heat, deseed the chilli.

a glug of olive oil
1 teaspoon cumin seeds
1 onion, roughly chopped
1 red pepper, deseeded and roughly chopped into 1cm pieces
1 red chilli, finely chopped
2 garlic cloves, finely chopped
1 teaspoon ground cumin
1 teaspoon ground coriander
1 teaspoon paprika
400g tin chopped tomatoes
1 x OXO Vegetable Stock Cube, made up with 500ml boiling water
240g tin black beans, drained and rinsed
240g tin kidney beans, drained and rinsed
175g tin black-eyed beans, drained and rinsed
sea salt

To serve
fresh coriander leaves
sour cream
grated Cheddar cheese
2–3 corn tortillas per person
guacamole

1 Heat the oil in a large saucepan, add the cumin seeds and fry over a low heat for 1 minute until aromatic. Add the onion, red pepper, chilli and garlic. Stir and fry over a medium to low heat for 5 minutes, until softened.

2 Lower the heat and add the ground cumin, coriander and paprika. Fry for 1 minute until aromatic, then add the tomatoes, OXO stock and all the beans and stir well. Bring to the boil and simmer, uncovered, for 15–30 minutes, depending on how much time you have.

3 Add salt to taste, then top with coriander, sour cream and grated Cheddar, and serve with the tortillas and guacamole, with everyone assembling their own fajitas.

ox

4

POT ROASTS

ONE POT
ROAST BEEF

This makes a great, hands-off alternative to the more traditional Sunday roast; it looks after itself in the oven, and because it doesn't call for any last-minute vegetable or gravy preparation, couldn't be easier.

900g–1kg beef topside joint
a big glug of olive oil
1 onion, cut into 8 wedges
1 x OXO Rich Beef with Onion & Rosemary Stock Pot, made up with 450ml boiling water
1 x OXO Rosemary & Thyme Herbs & More
350g turnips, cut into generous 2.5cm chunks
350g potatoes, peeled and cut into generous 2.5cm chunks
200g carrots, cut into 2.5cm chunks
250g swede, peeled and cut into generous 2.5cm chunks
sea salt and freshly ground black pepper

1 Preheat the oven to 150°C/gas 2. Season the beef all over with salt and pepper and rub it well with the olive oil.

2 Heat a deep flameproof casserole, large enough to hold the meat and vegetables snugly, and add the beef. Sear it well over a high heat for 3 minutes on each side until well browned, then remove to a dish.

3 Add the onion and OXO stock to the pan, then stir in the OXO Rosemary & Thyme Herbs & More. Bubble for a few minutes, stirring well to scrape up any sediment from the bottom of the pan.

4 Add the turnips, potatoes, carrots and swede, and season well with salt and pepper. Place the beef on top, arranging the vegetables so that two thirds of the beef is submerged in the cooking liquid.

5 Cover with a lid and transfer to the oven. Cook for 3 hours, turning the joint over after 1 hour 30 minutes.

6 Remove the beef to a board and taste the broth, adding salt and pepper if needed. Carve the beef into slices and serve with the broth and vegetables.

POT ROAST LAMB SHOULDER WITH CANNELLINI BEANS

Lamb and creamy white beans are a classic combination, for good reason, and this slow-cook, succulent Italian-inspired dish makes a fine centrepiece for a shared meal with family and friends. Serve with a mustardy green salad and crusty bread to mop up the rich, garlicky juices.

1kg boneless lamb shoulder
a big glug of olive oil
2–3 fresh rosemary sprigs
10 garlic cloves, left unpeeled and bashed
1 onion, roughly sliced
150ml white wine
1 x OXO Lamb Stock Cube, made up with
75ml boiling water
400g tin chopped tomatoes
400g tin cannellini beans, drained and rinsed
sea salt and freshly ground black pepper

1 Preheat the oven to 150°C/gas 2. Rub the lamb all over with the oil and a good scattering of salt and pepper.

2 Heat the oil in a large flameproof casserole and add the lamb. Sear it well for 3–4 minutes on each side until well browned all over. Add the rosemary, garlic and onion and turn the lamb over so the best side is facing upwards.

3 Add the wine and allow it to bubble down well for a few minutes, before adding the OXO stock, tomatoes and drained cannellini beans. Season well with salt and pepper and stir the beans and tomatoes together gently.

4 Bring to the boil, cover and transfer immediately to the oven to cook for 3 hours, removing the lid for the final 45 minutes of cooking. Remove the lamb to a board to carve into slices, and serve the beans and juices separately.

POT ROAST
CHICKEN

Pot-roasting in liquid keeps the chicken beautifully moist and succulent and gives you a rich and flavourful gravy. With the veg all cooked in the pot too, it only leaves potatoes to prepare as an accompaniment. Perfect for a weekend family lunch.

a big glug of olive oil
1.6kg whole chicken
½ lemon
150ml dry cider
300g parsnips, peeled and cut into large chunks
200g carrots, peeled and cut into large chunks
5–6 garlic cloves, left unpeeled and bashed
6 shallots, peeled and halved
1 x OXO Rosemary & Thyme Herbs & More
1 x OXO Succulent Chicken with Garlic & Thyme Stock Pot, made up with 350ml boiling water
sea salt and freshly ground black pepper

1 Preheat the oven to 180°C/gas 4. Heat half the oil in a large flameproof casserole or stock pot, large enough to comfortably hold the chicken and all the vegetables.

2 Rub the chicken all over with the remaining oil and some salt and pepper, and place the lemon half in the cavity.

3 Put the chicken breast side down in the casserole and fry over a high heat for 3 minutes on each side until the chicken is evenly golden brown all over. Sit the chicken breast side up, then pour in the cider and let it bubble for 3–4 minutes.

4 Tuck all the parsnips, carrots, garlic and shallots around the chicken in the casserole. Dissolve the OXO Rosemary & Thyme Herbs & More in the hot OXO stock. Pour half the OXO stock into the cavity of the chicken and the other half over the veg.

5 Bring to the boil, then cover with a lid and transfer immediately to the oven. Cook for 1 hour 30 minutes, then, if you prefer the gravy to be more intense and rich rather than broth-like, remove the chicken and vegetables to a large platter and cover with foil to keep warm. Place the casserole on the hob and reduce the cooking liquid over a high heat for 10 minutes. Add salt and pepper to taste and serve alongside the chicken.

MOROCCAN LAMB SHANKS WITH CHICKPEAS

This fragrant, succulent dish is ideal for a dinner party, its slow, hands-off cooking time in the oven leaving you free to get on with other preparations. Serve with couscous.

a big glug of olive oil
4 lamb shanks
3 onions, finely sliced
4 garlic cloves, grated
a small knob of fresh ginger, peeled and grated
2 teaspoons ground cumin
2 teaspoons ground coriander
1 teaspoon cayenne
1 x OXO Lamb Stock Cube, made up with 250ml boiling water
400g tin chopped tomatoes
2 x 400g tins chickpeas, drained and rinsed
2 bay leaves
sea salt and freshly ground black pepper

1 Preheat the oven to 150°C/gas 2.

2 Heat the oil in a large flameproof casserole and, working in batches, sear the lamb shanks for 3 minutes on each side until well browned all over. Transfer to a plate.

3 Add the onions to the casserole and cook over a medium to high heat for 10 minutes until golden brown, stirring occasionally. Reduce the heat and add the grated garlic, ginger, cumin, coriander and cayenne.

4 Fry for 2–3 minutes until aromatic, before adding the OXO stock, tomatoes, chickpeas and bay leaves.

5 Return the lamb shanks to the casserole with a good pinch of salt and pepper. Stir and bring to the boil, then cover and transfer immediately to the oven. Cook for 2 hours 30 minutes, then serve hot.

ox

PIES AND HOTPOTS

CHICKEN, LEEK AND HAM PIE

Pies are always popular with young and old alike, and this one makes an ideal family supper dish, served either with peas, or a salad in summer.

½ onion, roughly chopped
1 carrot, roughly chopped
1 celery stick, roughly chopped
2 x OXO Succulent Chicken with Garlic & Thyme Stock Pots, made up with 850ml boiling water
750g chicken thighs and drumsticks
a glug of olive oil
20g butter
700g leeks, thinly sliced
200g cooked ham, chopped
150ml double cream
a big squeeze of lemon juice, or to taste
320g ready-rolled puff pastry
1 egg, beaten
sea salt and freshly ground black pepper

1 Put the onion, carrot and celery in a large stock pot and add the OXO stock. Bring to the boil, add the chicken thighs and drumsticks and reduce the heat to a bare simmer. Cook for 35 minutes, then remove the cooked chicken and, when cool enough to handle, strip the meat from the bones, discarding the skin. Boil the poaching stock over a high heat to a third of its original volume.

2 Meanwhile, heat the oil and butter in a large frying pan over a low heat. Add the leeks, stir, cover and cook for 10 minutes until softened.

3 Add the reduced stock, cooked chicken, ham and cream to the leeks and stir well, adding a big squeeze of lemon juice and a pinch of salt and pepper to taste.

4 Transfer the mixture to a large pie dish and set aside to cool a little while you preheat the oven to 200°C/gas 6.

5 Brush the edges of the pie dish with some beaten egg and cover with the pastry, trimming as necessary. Crimp the edges of the pastry using a fork, cut a small cross in the middle and brush all over with beaten egg. Bake in oven for 30 minutes until the pastry is golden brown.

BEEF, RED WINE AND ROSEMARY HOT POT

The delicious, golden potato topping makes this dish a meal in itself, but you can serve it with a green vegetables for colour and a health boost, if you like. Perfect for a cold winter's evening.

a big glug of olive oil
400g diced stewing steak
2 tablespoons plain flour
150ml red wine
150g carrots, cut into 1cm dice
1 onion, roughly chopped
100g celery, cut into 1cm chunks
1 x OXO Rosemary & Red Wine Herbs & More
1 x OXO Rich Beef with Onion & Rosemary Stock Pot, made up with 200ml boiling water
400g floury potatoes, such as Maris Piper, thinly sliced
10g butter
sea salt and freshly ground black pepper

1 Preheat the oven to 150°C/gas 2. Heat half the oil in a large frying pan. Season the steak all over with salt and pepper and dust well with the flour.

2 Working in 2 batches, fry the beef for a few minutes on all sides over a high heat until well browned all over. Transfer to a casserole or oven dish that has a lid. Pour the wine into the frying pan and let it bubble for a few minutes, to deglaze, before pouring it over the beef.

3 Heat the remaining oil in the frying pan and add the carrots, onion and celery. Pour in the OXO Rosemary & Red Wine Herbs & More. Stir well and cook over a medium to low heat for 10 minutes, stirring occasionally, until the vegetables are softened. Transfer to the casserole dish containing the beef and wine.

4 Pour the OXO stock over the beef and vegetables, stir and add salt and pepper to taste. Arrange the potato slices in overlapping layers on top, seasoning between each layer.

5 Dot the potatoes with the butter, put the lid on and cook in the oven for 1 hour 45 minutes. Remove the lid, increase the oven temperature to 180°C/gas 4 and cook for a further 45 minutes, until the potatoes are golden brown and crisp.

LEEK AND MUSHROOM POT PIES (V)

Everyone loves a pie, and it's always good to have a delicious vegetarian version you can offer to friends or family. The creamy leeks and mushrooms make these every bit as comforting and satisfying as a traditional meat pie. Serve with a green salad or veg.

a big glug of olive oil
800g leeks, sliced
4 garlic cloves, finely chopped
700g chestnut mushrooms, roughly chopped
1 x OXO Garden Vegetables with Parsley & Bay Stock Pot, made up with 300ml boiling water
200ml double cream
1 x OXO Lemon & Thyme Herbs & More
320g ready-rolled puff pastry
1 egg, lightly beaten
sea salt and freshly ground black pepper

1 Preheat the oven to 200°C/gas 6.

2 Heat the oil in a large frying pan and add the leeks and garlic. Cook for 5 minutes to soften, then add the mushrooms and cook for a further 5 minutes, stirring frequently. Add the OXO stock and bubble down for 2 minutes before adding the cream and bubbling down for 2 minutes. Stir in the OXO Lemon & Thyme Herbs & More. Remove from the heat and season well with a pinch of salt and pepper.

3 Divide the mushroom and leek mixture equally between 4 small pie dishes or pots and allow to cool for 5 minutes.

4 Cut out pastry squares or circles just larger than the top of each dish, and brush the edges of each dish with the beaten egg before sticking the pastry over the top. Trim the edges of the pastry with a sharp knife and cut a small hole in the middle of each pie to allow the steam to escape. (For a bit of fun, you could make pastry 'O's and place one on either side of an 'X'-shaped steam hole, as in the picture opposite.) Crimp the edges of each pie with a fork or gently scallop the edges, then brush the tops with the beaten egg.

5 Cook the pies in the oven for 25 minutes, before serving hot.

PORK, LEEK AND MUSTARD CASSEROLE WITH HERBY DUMPLINGS

The herby dumplings transform this succulent casserole into comfort food at its best – perfect for a cold winter's evening or weekend family lunch.

800g diced pork shoulder
2 tablespoons plain flour
3 tablespoons olive oil
300ml white wine
700g leeks, thinly sliced
80g celery, thinly sliced
4 garlic cloves, finely chopped
4 tablespoons chopped fresh tarragon
4 tablespoons Dijon mustard
1 x OXO Succulent Chicken with Garlic & Thyme Stock Pot, made up with 500ml boiling water
sea salt and freshly ground black pepper

For the dumplings
400g plain flour
2 teaspoons baking powder
110g butter, diced
2 x OXO Roast Garlic & Parsley Herbs & More
100ml hot water from the kettle
pinch of sea salt

1 Preheat the oven to 160°C/gas 3. Dust the pork all over with the flour and season with salt and pepper.

2 Heat 1 tablespoon of the oil in a large frying pan. Working in batches, fry the meat for 2 minutes each side until well browned, before removing to a bowl, adding another tablespoon of oil as necessary. Add the wine to the pan and let it bubble down for a couple of minutes, scraping up any sediment on the base using a wooden spoon. Pour the contents of the pan over the pork.

3 Heat the remaining oil in a large flameproof casserole and add the leeks, celery and garlic. Stir, cover and cook over a medium heat for 6–7 minutes until softened. Add the tarragon and mustard and stir.

4 Add the pork to the casserole with the OXO stock. Season with salt and pepper and stir well. Bring to the boil, cover with the lid and transfer immediately to the oven to cook for 1 hour 30 minutes.

5 To make the dumplings, rub the flour, baking powder and butter together until it resembles sand. Mix the OXO Roast Garlic & Parsley Herbs & More with the water, then pour it into the flour mixture with the salt. Bring together into a dough and form 8 dumplings. Remove the lid from the casserole at the end of cooking and arrange the dumplings over the casserole. Return to the oven, uncovered, for 30 minutes until the dumplings are golden and cooked.

SHEPHERD'S PIE

Traditionally made from leftover roast lamb, this updated version uses lamb mince, with the rosemary adding complementary herby notes. A classic family supper dish, this can be prepared in advance before its final oven cook, making it very adaptable to busy schedules.

a glug of olive oil
425g lamb mince
1 onion, finely chopped
2 garlic cloves, finely chopped
1 tablespoon tomato purée
1 x OXO Rosemary & Thyme Herbs & More
1 x OXO Lamb Stock Cube, made up with
600ml boiling water
500g potatoes, peeled and cut into 2.5cm chunks
10g butter
50ml milk
sea salt and freshly ground black pepper

1 Heat half the oil in a large frying pan, add the mince and fry for 10 minutes over a medium to high heat, breaking it up well with a wooden spoon, then stirring occasionally until well browned and crisp. You may need to do this in 2 batches to avoid overcrowding the pan.

2 Tip the browned mince into a sieve set over a bowl to drain off the excess fat. Return 1 tablespoon of the lamb fat to the frying pan and add the onion and garlic.

3 Fry for 10 minutes over a low heat, partially covered and stirring occasionally, until softened. Return the mince to the pan and add the tomato purée. Stir well, then add the OXO Rosemary & Thyme Herbs & More and the OXO stock, stir, bring to the boil and simmer gently, uncovered, for 35 minutes.

4 Meanwhile, preheat the oven to 180°C/gas 4. Put the potatoes into a large pan of cold water and bring to the boil. Cook at a rolling boil for 15 minutes until cooked through, then drain well and leave to steam-dry for 5 minutes.

5 Return the potatoes to the saucepan and mash well. Add the butter and milk and mix well until smooth. Add salt and pepper to taste to the potatoes and the lamb mixture, then transfer the lamb to an ovenproof dish.

6 Pipe or spread the mashed potato on top, drizzle with the remaining tablespoon of oil, grind over some pepper and cook on the top shelf of the oven for 35–40 minutes until golden brown and bubbling round the edges.

ox

6

PASTA

LINGUINE WITH CHERRY TOMATOES, MUSHROOMS, PARSLEY AND CREAM (V)

This creamy, luxurious pasta dish uses readily available ingredients and takes no time at all to prepare, making it perfect for a midweek supper when time is short and energy levels low.

200g linguine
a big glug of olive oil
2 garlic cloves, chopped
250g chestnut mushrooms, quartered
150g cherry tomatoes, halved
75ml double cream
1 x OXO Lemon & Thyme Herbs & More
a big squeeze of lemon juice
a big handful of fresh flat-leaf parsley, finely chopped
sea salt and freshly ground black pepper
freshly grated Parmesan, to serve

1 Bring a large pan of salted water to the boil. Add the linguine and cook until al dente, according to the packet instructions (about 10–12 minutes). Drain, reserving 2 ladlefuls of the cooking water.

2 Meanwhile, while the pasta water is coming to the boil, heat the oil in a large frying pan and add the garlic. Gently fry over a low heat for 1 minute before increasing the heat and adding the mushrooms. Fry for 5–6 minutes.

3 Add the cherry tomatoes and fry for 3–4 minutes until the tomatoes have softened slightly. Lower the heat and stir through the cream and OXO Lemon & Thyme Herbs & More. Remove from the heat and stir through a big squeeze of lemon juice and the parsley.

4 Tip the drained linguine into the pan with the mushrooms and tomatoes and mix well to thoroughly coat in the sauce, adding a little of the reserved cooking water as needed to loosen. Add a pinch of salt and pepper to taste and serve immediately, with Parmesan grated over the top.

SPAGHETTI WITH SMOKED SALMON, LEMON AND DILL

The classic combination of smoked salmon and dill turns simple pasta into an elegant but fantastically quick and easy lunch or supper dish.

200g spaghetti
1 x OXO Lemon & Thyme Herbs & More
15g butter
120g smoked salmon, cut or torn into strips
a big handful of fresh dill, roughly chopped
freshly ground black pepper

1 Bring a large pan of salted water to the boil and cook the spaghetti until al dente, according to the packet instructions (about 10–12 minutes). Drain, reserving a ladleful of the cooking water.

2 Return the drained spaghetti to the pan and mix through the OXO Lemon & Thyme Herbs & More and the butter, until both are fully melted.

3 Stir in the smoked salmon and dill, adding the reserved pasta water a little at a time if the pasta looks dry. Add a pinch of pepper to taste and serve immediately.

Cook's Tip: Stir in a couple of dollops of crème fraîche with the salmon and dill, if you like.

RIGATONI WITH QUICK-COOK RAGU

Even if you're in a hurry, cooking the various elements in several frying pans means you can still make this delicious Bolognese-style ragu. If you have more time, simmer the ragu in a saucepan for up to an hour, which will give an even richer taste.

3 tablespoons olive oil
3 garlic cloves, finely chopped
1 x OXO Rosemary & Red Wine Herbs & More
2 x 400g tins chopped tomatoes
1 x OXO Rich Beef with Onion & Rosemary
Stock Pot, made up with 500ml boiling water
2 onions, finely chopped
400g beef mince
400g rigatoni
sea salt and freshly ground black pepper
freshly shaved Parmesan, to serve

1 Heat 1 tablespoon of the oil in a large frying pan and add the garlic. Fry for a minute, then add the OXO Rosemary & Red Wine Herbs & More, tomatoes and OXO stock. Stir well, then bring to the boil and allow the sauce to bubble away over a medium heat.

2 Meanwhile, heat another 1 tablespoon of the oil in a second large frying pan and add the onions. Fry over a medium heat for 5 minutes, until browned around the edges, then tip into the tomato sauce.

3 Heat the remaining 1 tablespoon oil in the frying pan used for the onions and, working in batches, fry off the mince for about 10 minutes, until nicely browned all over, breaking it up well with a wooden spoon as you go. Tip into the tomato sauce and simmer for 10–15 minutes until well reduced.

4 Meanwhile, bring a large pan of salted water to the boil and cook the rigatoni until al dente, according to the packet instructions (about 10–12 minutes). Drain, reserving a ladleful of the pasta water.

5 Stir the pasta through the ragu, then taste and add salt and pepper to taste, stirring in a little of the reserved pasta water to loosen the sauce if needed. Serve sprinkled with Parmesan shavings, if using.

PENNE WITH ITALIAN ROAST VEGETABLE SAUCE (V)

For a quick, healthy midweek dinner that's packed with flavour, this roast vegetable pasta dish is the perfect option.

1 aubergine, cut into 1cm chunks
1 red pepper, cut into 1cm chunks
1 red onion, roughly chopped
4 garlic cloves, left unpeeled and bashed
3 tablespoons olive oil
1 x OXO Rosemary & Thyme Herbs & More
2 x 400g tins chopped tomatoes
400g penne
a glug of extra virgin olive oil
sea salt and freshly ground black pepper
freshly grated Parmesan, to serve (optional)

1 Preheat the oven to 200°C/gas 6. Place the chopped aubergine, pepper, onion and the garlic cloves in a single layer in a roasting tin, season with salt and pepper and drizzle with 2 tablespoons of the olive oil. Mix well, then roast on the highest shelf in the oven for 25 minutes.

2 Heat the remaining tablespoon of oil in a deep pan, add the OXO Rosemary & Thyme Herbs & More and stir to melt. Add the tomatoes, stir well, then bring to the boil and simmer for 20 minutes.

3 While the sauce is simmering, bring a large stock pot of salted water to the boil and cook the penne until slightly al dente, according to the packet instructions (about 10–12 minutes). Drain, reserving a ladleful of the cooking liquid.

4 Tip the drained pasta back into the stock pot with the roasted vegetables, add the tomato sauce and gently stir together. Add a pinch of salt and pepper to taste, stirring in a little of the reserved cooking liquid if needed. Stir through the extra virgin olive oil to finish and serve immediately, sprinkled with grated Parmesan if you like.

TAGLIATELLE WITH COURGETTE, FETA AND SPRING ONIONS (V)

The flavours in this simple pasta dish are so fresh and light, making it a perfect summer lunch or supper, either served with a green salad or just as it is.

400g tagliatelle
a big glug of olive oil
3 garlic cloves, finely chopped
6 spring onions, finely sliced
½ red chilli, finely chopped
1 x OXO Lemon & Thyme Herbs & More
3 courgettes, grated
100g feta cheese, crumbled
a big squeeze of lemon juice, or to taste
sea salt and freshly ground black pepper

1 Bring a large pan of salted water to the boil and cook the tagliatelle until al dente, according to the packet instructions (about 10–12 minutes). Drain, reserving a ladleful of the cooking water.

2 Meanwhile, heat the oil in a large frying pan and add the garlic, spring onions and chilli. Fry for 1–2 minutes, then add the OXO Lemon & Thyme Herbs & More and stir until melted.

3 Add the grated courgette and fry for about 6–7 minutes until wilted.

4 Stir the drained pasta through the courgette mixture and add the feta. Add a big squeeze of lemon juice and a pinch of salt and pepper to taste, and loosen the mixture with the reserved pasta water if needed. Serve immediately.

FUSILLI WITH SQUASH, GOAT'S CHEESE, MUSHROOMS AND SAGE (V)

The fried sage leaves add a wonderful crunch and dash of green to this gorgeous, colourful dish. If not serving immediately, it makes an excellent warm pasta salad.

a big glug of olive oil
24 fresh sage leaves
1 x OXO Roast Garlic & Parsley Herbs & More
750g butternut squash, peeled, deseeded and cut into 1cm chunks
250g chestnut mushrooms, halved if large
400g fusilli
120g goat's cheese, roughly chopped
sea salt and freshly ground black pepper

1 Heat the oil in a large frying pan and add the sage leaves. Fry over a medium to high heat for 1–2 minutes until crisp, then remove with a slotted spoon and set aside on a plate.

2 Add the OXO Roast Garlic & Parsley Herbs & More and butternut squash to the sage-infused oil in the pan and fry for a minute until the Herbs & More has melted. Lower the heat slightly, then cover and cook for 10 minutes. Add the mushrooms, gently stir to mix, then cook, uncovered, for a further 10 minutes until the mushrooms are cooked through.

3 Meanwhile, bring a large pan of salted water to the boil and cook the fusilli until al dente, according to the packet instructions (about 12–13 minutes). Drain, reserving a ladleful of the cooking water.

4 Tip the drained pasta into the mushroom and squash mixture along with the goat's cheese, and mix well, adding the reserved pasta water as required if the pasta looks dry. Add a pinch of salt and pepper to taste, then top with the reserved crispy sage leaves.

ox

7

SIDES AND SAUCES

ROAST VEGETABLE COUSCOUS (V)

Like the Easy Egg Fried Rice on page 107, this works well as a meal in itself as well as a perfect accompaniment to meat or fish dishes. Any leftovers work brilliantly in a lunchbox the next day.

1 aubergine, cut into 1cm chunks
1 red pepper, deseeded and cut into 1cm chunks
1 red onion, cut into 1cm chunks
a big glug of olive oil
1 x OXO Vegetable Stock Cube, made up with 300ml boiling water
240g quick-cook couscous
a big squeeze of lemon juice, or to taste
sea salt and freshly ground black pepper

1 Preheat the oven to 200°C/gas 6.

2 In a large roasting tin, toss the aubergine, pepper and onion with the oil and a good pinch of salt. Transfer to the oven and roast for 25 minutes until all the vegetables are lightly charred and cooked through.

3 Ten minutes before the vegetables are ready, bring the OXO stock to the boil in a small pan. Place the couscous in a heatproof bowl and pour the boiling OXO stock over it. Cover with a plate and leave for 5 minutes, for the couscous to absorb the stock, then remove the plate and leave for a further minute before fluffing through the couscous with a fork.

4 Tip the couscous into the roasting tin with the vegetables and stir well. Return to the oven for 3–4 minutes to allow the couscous to absorb the flavour of the vegetables, then add a big squeeze of lemon juice and a pinch of salt and pepper to taste, before serving hot or warm.

CASHEW NUT PILAF (V)

This lightly spiced, nutty rice dish makes a delicious alternative to plain rice – a perfect accompaniment to Chicken Jalfrezi (page 57), Lamb Keema Curry (page 58) or Chickpea and Coriander Curry (page 55).

20g butter
1 bay leaf
6 cardamom pods
1 cinnamon stick
6 cloves
70g cashew nuts
300g basmati rice, rinsed well in cold water
1 x OXO Vegetable Stock Cube, made up with 750ml boiling water
300ml boiling water

1 Heat the butter in a large saucepan until foaming, then reduce the heat and add the bay leaf, cardamom pods, cinnamon stick and cloves. Fry for 2 minutes until aromatic, then add the cashew nuts and fry for 2–3 minutes until golden brown.

2 Add the rice and fry for 1 minute, then add the OXO stock and boiling water. Bring to the boil, stir well, then reduce to a very low simmer, cover with a tight-fitting lid and reduce the heat to as low as possible.

3 Cook for 15 minutes without removing the lid, then remove from the heat and fluff the rice through with a fork. Set aside to steam-dry for 5 minutes before serving. (You could do this by spreading it out on 2 large plates.)

EASY EGG FRIED RICE (V)

This works as a side with a range of dishes, particularly Asian, but is also delicious as a meal in itself, just as it is here. Feel free to add strips of cooked chicken or extra veg, such as baby corn.

400g basmati rice
1 x OXO Vegetable Stock Cube, made up with 750ml boiling water
500ml water
2 garlic cloves, left unpeeled
30g butter
2 teaspoons whole black peppercorns
3 eggs, lightly beaten
150g defrosted frozen peas
3 tablespoons soy sauce

1 Rinse the rice well in several changes of cold water, then put into a saucepan that has a tight-fitting lid. Add the OXO stock, water and garlic and bring to the boil. Reduce the heat to the lowest possible setting, cover and leave to steam for 15 minutes without removing the lid.

2 Remove from the heat and leave to steam-dry for 5 minutes (or spread it out on two large plates if you prefer).

3 Meanwhile, heat the butter in a large frying pan until foaming. Add the peppercorns and fry for 2 minutes until aromatic. Add the eggs and briefly scramble over a medium heat for 2 minutes before adding the rice.

4 Fry the rice and eggs together for 2–3 minutes, then add the peas and cook for a further minute. Stir through the soy sauce, then taste and season with more soy sauce, if needed. Serve hot.

GLAZED CARROTS WITH LEMON AND THYME (V)

This method of cooking carrots in their own steam allows them to retain all their flavour, and also gives a lovely twist to the usual boiled method of cooking.

20g butter
1 x OXO Lemon & Thyme Herbs & More
450g carrots, sliced 1cm thick, in rounds or on the diagonal
1 tablespoon water
black pepper

1 Heat the butter in a heavy-based saucepan until foaming. Add the OXO Lemon & Thyme Herbs & More and stir until just melted. Add the carrots and stir well to coat, then cover and cook for 5 minutes.

2 Remove the lid and add the water to the pan, then shake well. Cover again and cook for 10 minutes, shaking the pan halfway through. Add pepper to taste before serving.

FRENCH-STYLE GREEN VEGETABLES
WITH GARLIC, SHALLOTS AND MINT (V)

Our way of serving these sweet summer veg, with added interest from the stock and herbs, adds a twist of flavour to turn them into something more special. They are perfect served alongside roasts or meat dishes, or with an omelette or cheese dish for a lunch with friends.

220g green beans, trimmed
12 baby shallots, peeled and halved
200g sugar snap peas
100g defrosted frozen peas
20g butter
1 x OXO Roast Garlic & Parsley Herbs & More
a big handful of fresh mint leaves, finely chopped
a big squeeze of lemon juice, or to taste
sea salt and freshly ground black pepper

1 Bring a very large pan of salted water to the boil, add the green beans and shallots and boil for 1 minute, before adding the sugar snaps. Boil for a further 2 minutes before adding the peas. Drain well before plunging all the vegetables into a bowl of cold water to arrest the cooking.

2 Melt the butter in a large frying pan and add the OXO Roast Garlic & Parsley Herbs & More. Stir well until evenly melted. Drain the cooled vegetables well and tip them into the pan.

3 Fry the vegetables for 1 minute until heated through and well coated in the herb butter. Stir through the mint and add a big squeeze of lemon juice and a pinch of salt and pepper to taste before serving hot.

GRIDDLED ASPARAGUS (V)

This makes a really delicious starter or side dish, perfect for serving during the asparagus season in May and June when the vegetable is at its very best. Griddling brings out the flavour and adds texture, keeping the stems nice and firm.

400g asparagus, woody ends trimmed
a glug of olive oil
1 tablespoon butter
1 x OXO Lemon & Thyme Herbs & More
freshly ground black pepper

1 Bring a large pan of salted water to the boil. Drop the asparagus in and blanch for 1 minute, then remove immediately to a bowl of iced water. Drain the cooled asparagus and toss with the olive oil.

2 Melt the butter in a small saucepan, add the OXO Lemon & Thyme Herbs & More and stir to dissolve, adding a couple of teaspoons of water for a thinner sauce, if required.

3 Heat a large griddle pan until smoking, then, working in batches, add the asparagus and griddle for 1 minute on each side, until you have nice char marks on both sides. Drizzle over the sauce, add a pinch of pepper to taste and serve hot.

CHEESY POTATO GRATIN (V)

This comforting dish makes a perfect accompaniment to the Pork, Cider and Apple Stew on page 39, or to a winter roast. Served with a seasonal salad, it is also delicious as a stand-alone dish at any time of year.

1kg floury potatoes, such as Maris Piper, peeled and thinly sliced
20g butter, cut into small cubes
1 x OXO Roast Garlic & Parsley Herbs & More
2 tablespoons Dijon mustard
100ml full-fat milk
100g strong Cheddar cheese, grated
30g white breadcrumbs
sea salt and freshly ground black pepper

1 Preheat the grill to high.

2 Bring a large pan of water to the boil and add the sliced potatoes. Return to the boil and cook for 10–12 minutes until tender when pierced with a sharp knife.

3 Drain well and allow the potatoes to steam dry for a minute, before returning to the pan and mashing well until smooth. Stir through the butter, OXO Roast Garlic & Parsley Herbs & More, mustard, milk and half the grated cheese. Add salt and pepper to taste.

4 Spread the potatoes out in a baking dish and sprinkle the remaining grated cheese and breadcrumbs evenly over the top. Add a grind of pepper, then flash under the grill for 3–4 minutes until the topping is golden brown and nicely crisp. Serve hot.

LONG-STEM BROCCOLI WITH LEMON AND THYME (V)

This curiously addictive vegetable dish goes with just about anything you can think of, and is super healthy too.

400g long-stem broccoli
1 tablespoon butter
1 x OXO Lemon & Thyme Herbs & More
freshly ground black pepper

1 Bring a large pan of salted water to the boil. Add the broccoli and cook for 3–5 minutes, depending on how firm you like it.

2 Drain in a colander, then add the butter and OXO Lemon & Thyme Herbs & More to the pan. Heat until just melted, then return the drained broccoli to the pan and stir well to coat. Add pepper to taste and serve hot.

ULTIMATE HERBY CAULIFLOWER CHEESE (V)

This makes a great accompaniment to roasts, but can equally be served as a dish in its own right, perhaps balanced with a green vegetable or salad, or even a tray of slow-roast tomatoes.

1 large cauliflower, cut into medium-sized florets
30g butter
2 heaped tablespoons plain flour
500ml hot milk
1 heaped tablespoon Dijon mustard
1 x OXO Rosemary & Thyme Herbs & More
100g strong Cheddar cheese, grated
30g breadcrumbs
sea salt and freshly ground black pepper

1 Bring a large pan of salted water to the boil and add the cauliflower. Partly cover and simmer for 8–10 minutes until just cooked but retaining some bite. Preheat the grill to its highest setting.

2 Meanwhile, melt the butter in a small saucepan over a medium to high heat until foaming. Add the flour and stir until the mixture comes together in a ball. You may need to add a little more flour, a teaspoon at a time, if the mixture is too liquid.

3 Stirring constantly, add the hot milk half a ladleful at a time, only adding the next after the previous ladleful has been incorporated. Continue until you have used up all the milk and have a smooth, lump-free sauce. Bring to the boil, stirring constantly, and cook for a further minute before removing from the heat. Add the mustard, OXO Rosemary & Thyme Herbs & More and 80g of the Cheddar and stir until smooth. Add salt and pepper to taste.

4 Arrange the cauliflower in one large or several smaller dishes and pour over the sauce. Sprinkle with the remaining Cheddar and the breadcrumbs, then flash under the hot grill for 2–3 minutes until golden brown and bubbling. Serve immediately.

GARLIC AND CHILLI KALE (V)

Leafy green kale is not only delicious, but is one of the healthiest vegetables around. The chilli and herbs in this recipe spice it up nicely. Serve as a side dish in winter, alongside casseroles or roasts.

a glug of olive oil
½ red chilli, finely chopped
1 x OXO Roast Garlic & Parsley Herbs & More
350g kale, roughly chopped

1 Heat the oil in a large saucepan over a medium to high heat, add the chilli and fry for 1 minute before adding the OXO Roast Garlic & Parsley Herbs & More. Stir to dissolve.

2 Add the kale and fry for 2 minutes to coat. Cover and cook for a further 2 minutes until wilted, then serve hot.

ROAST GARLIC AND PARSLEY GRAVY

This is the ideal gravy for roast chicken. If roasting your own, tip any cooking juices from the roasting tin into the gravy at the same time as adding the stock. For a richer sauce, stir through a heaped tablespoon of crème fraîche before serving.

15g butter
1 onion, finely chopped
1 x OXO Roast Garlic & Parsley Herbs & More
1 x OXO Succulent Chicken with Garlic & Thyme Stock Pot, made up with 400ml boiling water
freshly ground black pepper

1 Heat the butter in a medium saucepan until foaming, then add the onion. Stir, then cover and soften over a very low heat for 10 minutes, stirring occasionally.

2 Add the OXO Roast Garlic & Parsley Herbs & More and stir to melt. Pour over the OXO stock, bring to the boil then simmer, uncovered, for 15 minutes. Add a pinch of pepper to taste, then serve hot with roast chicken.

PERFECT ROSEMARY AND THYME GRAVY

Delicious with roast beef: add any cooking juices from your roasting tin to the gravy along with the stock. If you prefer a thicker gravy, instead of using plain flour, mix 1 tablespoon cornflour with 2 tablespoons water, and add to the pan along with the stock.

15g butter
1 red onion, finely sliced
1 tablespoon plain flour
1 x OXO Rosemary & Thyme Herbs & More
1 x OXO Rich Beef with Onion & Rosemary Stock Pot, made up with 500ml boiling water
freshly ground black pepper

1 Heat the butter in a medium saucepan until foaming, then add the red onion. Stir, then cover and soften over a low heat for 10 minutes.

2 Sprinkle in the flour and stir well to coat the onion. Add the OXO Rosemary & Thyme Herbs & More and stir until melted, then pour over the OXO stock.

3 Bring to the boil, then simmer, uncovered, for 15 minutes. Add a pinch of pepper to taste, then strain through a sieve into a jug and serve alongside a roast.

RED WINE, ROSEMARY AND ONION SAUCE

This intensely beefy, concentrated 'jus' is perfect for serving with steaks.

15g butter
1 red onion, finely sliced
1 x OXO Rosemary & Red Wine Herbs & More
1 x OXO Rich Beef with Onion & Rosemary Stock Pot, made up with 300ml boiling water
freshly ground black pepper

1 Heat the butter in a small pan until foaming, then add the onion. Fry over a medium heat for 5 minutes until golden brown at the edges.

2 Add the OXO Rosemary & Red Wine Herbs & More and stir until melted. Add the OXO stock, bring to the boil then simmer for 10 minutes. Add plenty of pepper and serve.

Cook's Tip: For added flavour, make this sauce in the pan that you used to cook your steaks, while your steaks rest on a warm plate under foil. Add the juices from the rested meat back into the sauce before serving.

LEMON, THYME AND SHALLOT SAUCE (V)

This sauce makes an excellent, simple accompaniment to all types of white fish.

15g butter
3 shallots, finely chopped
1 x OXO Lemon & Thyme Herbs & More
1 x OXO Garden Vegetables with Parsley & Bay Stock Pot, made up with 200ml boiling water
freshly ground black pepper

1 Heat the butter in a small saucepan until foaming. Add the shallots, stir, then cover and cook over a low heat for 10 minutes, until softened.

2 Stir through the OXO Lemon & Thyme Herbs & More until melted, then add the OXO stock. Bring to the boil then simmer for 10 minutes, until reduced. Add a pinch of pepper to taste and serve hot.

INDEX